How to use

• Five units — each with si×

This book is designed for discussion about wh.. ~~~~~~~~~~~~~~~~~ ~~~~ ~~~~ has six pages arranged as three double page spreads — each spread concentrates on a theme. You can look at the material on a page in any order and refer to it as you discuss.

• Headings and questions

Some questions are suggested as you go along, but I am sure that you will have plenty more of your own! There are tick-boxes at some points — there isn't always only one answer to these and you may wish to tick more than one.

• Coloured boxes

As well as the lilac coloured boxes with information and questions, there are yellow boxes

> **B**ible text from the NEW INTERNATIONAL VERSION
> *Bible reference*

with quotations from the New International Version of the Bible. In a group it is often helpful for somebody to read aloud from the book before you discuss that topic.

Christian belief
the bottom line
- **Main points from this double page spread**

• Summaries

At the end of each double page spread there is a grey box which aims to summarise the main points. You might be able to cover one unit in a session in which case you will complete the book in five sessions.

• I hope you enjoy the book

It is an impossible task to cover all aspects of the Christian faith in one small book and of course there are many shades of belief, but I hope that this will help you to understand the Christian message and to come to faith in Jesus Christ.

John Robertshaw

For more information on how to use this book in a church situation, see "Using Knock Knock!" available from Coastline Christian Resources.

God

- **What comes into your mind when you hear the word "God"?**

Which best represents your views?

- ☐ I do not believe that there is a God
- ☐ I think that there may be a God
- ☐ I wish I could believe in a God
- ☐ I believe that there is a God
- ☐ I have experienced God

Do you think God is:

- ☐ The creator
- ☐ A person
- ☐ Good
- ☐ Caring
- ☐ Other:

In the beginning God created the heavens and the earth. Now the earth was formless and empty, darkness was over the surface of the deep, and the Spirit of God was hovering over the waters. And God said, "Let there be light," and there was light. God saw that the light was good, and he separated the light from the darkness. God called the light "day", and the darkness he called "night". And there was evening, and there was morning—the first day.

Gen 1:1-5

Day 2   Water and sky separated
Day 3   Dry land, seas, vegetation, plants and trees
Day 4   Sun, moon and stars
Day 5   Fish and birds
Day 6   Animals and mankind

God saw all that he had made, and it was very good...Thus the heavens and the earth were completed in all their vast array.   *Gen 1:31-2:1*

- **What is your opinion of the Bible's description of creation?**

• But don't Scientists say that the universe started with a Big Bang about 10,000 million years ago?

Yes they do — this has been a popular scientific theory for a number of years now. You will find that Christians vary in their views of the age of the universe and exactly how it has developed since it was created. Science explains a lot about how the universe operates and the laws of nature but there are some questions it does not answer:

- **Where did everything come from?**

- **Why is the universe here and what is its purpose and significance?**

• Do you have answers to these questions?

> **T**hen the LORD answered... "Where were you when I laid the earth's foundation? Tell me, if you understand. Who marked off its dimensions? Surely you know! Who stretched a measuring line across it? On what were its footings set, or who laid its cornerstone?"
>
> *Job 38:4-6*
>
> The heavens declare the glory of God; the skies proclaim the work of his hands.
> *Psa 19:1*
>
> By faith we understand that the universe was formed at God's command, so that what is seen was not made out of what was visible.
> *Heb 11:3*

Christian belief
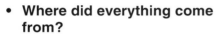

the bottom line

- **God is eternal, he has always existed and will continue for ever**

- **God exists independently from the universe**

- **God created everything, he is the only creator**

- **God made the universe out of nothing by his word of command**

- **God sustains the universe by his power**

• Design?

Scientists, artists and philosophers wonder at the beauty and complexity of the universe. Could all of this have happened without a designer?

• What do you think about Christian belief in God as creator?

God

• *God is a person!*

When we say that God is a person, we do not mean that he is a human being! We do mean that he is a personality: **someone**—not something, **he**—not it, **who**—not what. We cannot relate to a machine but we can relate to another free-thinking individual. God is not just an impersonal force behind the material universe but he is an eternal personality who longs for relationship with people.

The Bible at different times describes God as:
- Loving
- Caring
- Compassionate
- Glad
- Sad
- Angry
- Merciful
- Faithful
- Communicating
- Listening
- Aware of himself
- A father

Have you ever thought about God being a person before? What is your reaction?
- ☐ Surprised
- ☐ Sceptical
- ☐ Impressed
- ☐ Alarmed

Have you ever prayed?
- ☐ Yes
- ☐ No

If so — when? — and why?

Would you like to know God?
- ☐ Yes
- ☐ No
- ☐ Not sure

• *Love is more than just words!*

• *In what ways can you practically show that you love someone?*

• *God shows his love*

I will praise you, O Lord, among the nations; I will sing of you among the peoples. For great is your love, reaching to the heavens; your faithfulness reaches to the skies. *Psa 57:9-10*

The LORD is gracious and righteous; our God is full of compassion. *Psa 116:5*

You are forgiving and good, O Lord, abounding in love to all who call to you. Hear my prayer, O LORD; listen to my cry for mercy. In the day of my trouble I will call to you, for you will answer me. *Psa 86:7*

But God demonstrates his own love for us in this: While we were still sinners, Christ died for us. *Rom 5:8*

Christians believe that God's supreme act of love was the crucifixion of Jesus Christ — but more about that later.

J esus continued: "There was a man who had two sons. The younger one said to his father, 'Father, give me my share of the estate.' So he divided his property between them.

"Not long after that, the younger son got together all he had, set off for a distant country and there squandered his wealth in wild living. After he had spent everything, there was a severe famine in that whole country, and he began to be in need. So he went and hired himself out to a citizen of that country, who sent him to his fields to feed pigs. He longed to fill his stomach with the pods that the pigs were eating, but no one gave him anything.

"When he came to his senses, he said, 'How many of my father's hired men have food to spare, and here I am starving to death! I will set out and go back to my father and say to him: 'Father, I have sinned against heaven and against you. I am no longer worthy to be called your son; make me like one of your hired men.' So he got up and went to his father.

"But while he was still a long way off, his father saw him and was filled with compassion for him; he ran to his son, threw his arms around him and kissed him.

"The son said to him, 'Father, I have sinned against heaven and against you. I am no longer worthy to be called your son.'

"But the father said to his servants, 'Quick! Bring the best robe and put it on him. Put a ring on his finger and sandals on his feet. Bring the fattened calf and kill it. Let's have a feast and celebrate. For this son of mine was dead and is alive again; he was lost and is found.' So they began to celebrate."

Luke 15:11-24

This story is about a loving and forgiving father who accepts his wayward son back again. In the same way God longs to restore his relationship with us.

• *What would be your response to a son returning after squandering half of your wealth?*

Christian belief
the bottom line

- **God is a person to whom we can relate as a father**
- **God loves mankind**
- **God has shown his love through Jesus Christ**
- **God longs to restore his relationship with us**

God

• **Are there some things that you believe are absolutely right and absolutely wrong?**

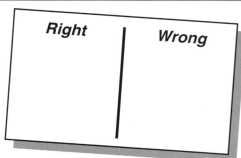

Right | Wrong

• **Why do you think these are right or wrong?**

• **God is good!**

Christians believe that God is in the best position to decide what is right and wrong. He is the ultimate judge of the whole universe and the only person able to establish absolute moral standards. Our own standards are not necessarily the same as God's standards. God himself is absolutely good and is incapable of doing wrong.

This is what the LORD says: "Let not the wise man boast of his wisdom or the strong man boast of his strength or the rich man boast of his riches, but let him who boasts boast about this: that he understands and knows me, that I am the LORD, who exercises kindness, justice and right-eousness on earth, for in these I delight," declares the LORD.　*Jer 9:23-24*

Some of God's standards

- Love God
- Don't worship idols
- Love other people
- Honour parents
- Do not murder
- No adultery
- No lying
- No jealousy
- No stealing
- No sexual immorality
- No blasphemy
- No selfishness

- No cheating
- No bribes
- No hate
- No occult activity
- No pride
- No greed
- Be generous
- Be humble
- Be kind
- Be patient
- Have mercy
- Be faithful

• **What is your opinion of God's standards?**

• If God is so good, why is there evil in the world?

Many people ask this question and some have sadly rejected God because of trouble in their own lives or in the world around them. Some understanding can be gained by considering **free choice**. Since God has given genuine free choice, there is necessarily the possibility of evil.

This does not mean that God is bad — in fact it shows that God is concerned to have a genuine relationship with his creation and that involves a risk! Nor does it mean that God isn't in control — he is all-powerful and can overrule at any time he wishes.

The Bible's explanation includes:

- **The existence of spiritual beings which have chosen an evil course (particularly the devil)**
- **The wayward nature of mankind**
- **The general fallen state of nature (more about this later)**

A central theme of Christianity is the defeat of evil

Christian belief
the bottom line

- *God is the ultimate judge of the universe*
- *He decides what is right and wrong*
- *He is good and can do no wrong*
- *Evil exists because of the existence of free choice*

Are all religions the same?

Some would say that all religions point to the same God. This is an over-simplification — if you look at other religions carefully you will find that there are considerable differences:

- The nature and character of God is so different. It can hardly be described as the same God.
- They have different views of the universe and God's relationship with it.
- They have different views of mankind and the way of salvation.

The God revealed in the Bible is the creator, he is personal, he is righteous, he loves mankind and he will be our judge.

• Have you learned anything new in this first unit?

Mankind

• Starting point

Scientists generally assume that life began spontaneously from the chemicals on this planet and that mankind evolved from simpler organisms by a process of "natural selection", involving mutation and survival of the fittest.

Many people seek to find their roots in nature and identify with the earth and with the plant and animal kingdom.

Do you believe that mankind is:

☐ The product of evolution

☐ Just an advanced animal

☐ Different from animals

☐ Made in the image of God

☐ Called to rule the earth

Do you believe that mankind is:

☐ Basically good

☐ Basically evil

☐ Good and bad

Why?

• The image of God

The Bible locates our roots first and foremost with God. Mankind alone is created in the image of God which carries with it certain responsibilities and privileges:

- **To rule over the earth and take care of it**

- **To have a special relationship with God**

- **A capacity for eternal life**

Although we are formed from the dust of the earth and are biologically similar to animals, we have a spiritual dimension since we are made in the image of God.

Then God said, "Let us make man in our image, in our likeness, and let them rule over the fish of the sea and the birds of the air, over the livestock, over all the earth, and over all the creatures that move along the ground."

So God created man in his own image, in the image of God he created him; male and female he created them.

God blessed them and said to them, "Be fruitful and increase in number; fill the earth and subdue it." *Gen 1:26-28*

The LORD God formed the man from the dust of the ground and breathed into his nostrils the breath of life, and the man became a living being. *Gen 2:7*

- ## Where do you think your roots are — on earth or in heaven? Why?

- ## The value of a soul

Biologically	Spiritually
God	God
———	Man
Man	
Animals	Animals
Plants	Plants
Earth	Earth

As human beings we have our own scale of values and some people seem more important than others, usually because of wealth or significant positions in this world. God has a different scale of values. All human beings are of great value to him, made in his image. There are no second class citizens with God. You are of great worth to God.

Consider the ravens: They do not sow or reap, they have no store-room or barn; yet God feeds them. And how much more valuable you are than birds!
Luke 12:24

How much more valuable is a man than a sheep!
Matt 12:12

Indeed, the very hairs of your head are all numbered. Don't be afraid; you are worth more than many sparrows.
Luke 12:7

- ## What do you think you are worth?

When I consider your heavens, the work of your fingers, the moon and the stars, which you have set in place, what is man that you are mindful of him, the son of man that you care for him?

You made him a little lower than the heavenly beings and crowned him with glory and honour.

You made him ruler over the works of your hands; you put everything under his feet: all flocks and herds, and the beasts of the field, the birds of the air, and the fish of the sea, all that swim the paths of the seas.

O LORD, our Lord, how majestic is your name in all the earth!
Psa 8:3-9

Christian belief
the bottom line

- Mankind is made in the image of God
- We are called to rule the earth and look after it
- Our roots are with God
- We are of great value to God

Mankind

• Spoilt image

It is clear that we are not how God originally intended us to be! Something has gone wrong and the image of God has somehow been spoilt and distorted.

The Bible's explanation goes back to early mankind which disobeyed God and became tragically separated from him. This situation has extended to the rest of the human race.

God

> **T**herefore, just as sin entered the world through one man, and death through sin, and in this way death came to all men, because all sinned...
> *Rom 5:12*
>
> Surely I was sinful at birth, sinful from the time my mother conceived me.
> *Psa 51:5*
>
> ...every inclination of his (man's) heart is evil from childhood. *Gen 8:21*
>
> For all have sinned and fall short of the glory of God. *Rom 3:23*
>
> We all, like sheep, have gone astray, each of us has turned to his own way...
> *Is 53:6*

> **A**nd the LORD God commanded the man, "You are free to eat from any tree in the garden; but you must not eat from the tree of the knowledge of good and evil, for when you eat of it you will surely die." *Gen 2:16-17*
>
> Now the serpent was more crafty than any of the wild animals the LORD God had made. He said to the woman, "Did God really say, 'You must not eat from any tree in the garden'?" ...
>
> When the woman saw that the fruit of the tree was good for food and pleasing to the eye, and also desirable for gaining wisdom, she took some and ate it. She also gave some to her husband, who was with her, and he ate it. Then the eyes of both of them were opened, and they realised that they were naked; so they sewed fig leaves together and made coverings for themselves.
>
> Then the man and his wife heard the sound of the LORD God as he was walking in the garden in the cool of the day, and they hid from the LORD God among the trees of the garden. But the LORD God called to the man, "Where are you?" *Gen 3:1-9*

Every area of mankind's existence has been spoilt — his physical well-being, his thinking, his moral judgment and his behaviour.

• What do you think of this explanation of the imperfections in mankind?

• *Paradise lost*

The state of mankind has affected the rest of nature. His rule over the earth is impaired and he struggles against the forces of nature. There is sickness, pollution, decay and catastrophe. His prospect of eternal life has also been lost.

> **C**ursed is the ground because of you; through painful toil you will eat of it all the days of your life. *Gen 3:17*
>
> We know that the whole creation has been groaning as in the pains of childbirth right up to the present time.
> *Rom 8:22*

• *Looking for the image*

Although mankind is fallen and separate from God, we do see traces of the image of God in genuine acts of compassion and love by our fellow man and in intellectual, practical and artistic achievements — but unfortunately it is tainted. We are like a beautiful symphony played by a very poor orchestra — the music is there, but distorted and not what the composer intended!

The Christian message is connected with recovering what has been lost and restoring the image of God in us.

• *When have you been impressed and when have you been disappointed by mankind?*

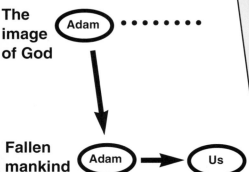

The image of God — Adam • • • • • • • •

Fallen mankind — Adam → Us

Christian belief
the bottom line

- Mankind has become separated from God by sin
- The image of God has been damaged and distorted
- Nature is also fallen and mankind's rule over it is impaired
- Eternal life has been lost

Mankind

• Destiny

Christians believe that God's interest in us as individuals began even before we were born, when he created us. He has a purpose for our lives and is concerned about our activities while here on this earth. He also cares about our eternal destiny.

• Do you believe that God has a purpose for your life?

• What do you think happens when you die?

> For you created my inmost being; you knit me together in my mother's womb. I praise you because I am fearfully and wonderfully made; your works are wonderful, I know that full well.
>
> My frame was not hidden from you when I was made in the secret place. When I was woven together in the depths of the earth, your eyes saw my unformed body.
>
> All the days ordained for me were written in your book before one of them came to be.   Psa 139:13-16
>
> "Before I formed you in the womb I knew you, before you were born I set you apart; I appointed you as a prophet to the nations."   Jer 1:5

Life beyond the grave is of importance to Christians. The Bible teaches that we will rise from the dead, be judged and that there will be a final division between the saved and the lost. The mission of Jesus Christ was to secure our eternal salvation.

> I tell you the truth, a time is coming and has now come when the dead will hear the voice of the Son of God and those who hear will live. For as the Father has life in himself, so he has granted the Son to have life in himself. And he has given him authority to judge because he is the Son of Man.
>
> Do not be amazed at this, for a time is coming when all who are in their graves will hear his voice and come out — those who have done good will rise to live, and those who have done evil will rise to be condemned.   John 5:25-29

Popular (non-Christian) theories about death

- **Annihilation** — when we die, we lose all consciousness and have no further existence; our bodies simply rot in the ground
- **Ghosts and spiritualism** — when we die, we enter a spirit world which may interact with the world of the living
- **Reincarnation** — when we die, we return to the earth in some other form
- **Optimism** — when we die, we all go to heaven

• Searching mankind

Men and women have always been searching for something — there is some gap in us that leads us to search for meaning and truth. Gods have been invented and philosophies have been devised to make sense of our existence. Modern man tries all sorts of ways to find meaning and fulfilment in this life.

Ways people try to find meaning and fulfilment in life:

- **Human relationships** — friendships and loving relationships
- **Religion** — ritual, meditation, good deeds, spiritual experiences
- **Intellect** — the pursuit of knowledge, the development of the mind, philosophy, scientific rational explanations
- **Arts** — music, literature, drama, poetry, films
- **Escapism** — television, fantasy, drugs, alcohol
- **Occult** — astrology, fortune telling, superstition, contacting the dead, magic
- **Pleasure** — wealth, material possessions, recreation, sport, sex

> **H**e has made everything beautiful in its time. He has also set eternity in the hearts of men; yet they cannot fathom what God has done from beginning to end. *Eccl 3:11*

• Where do you look for fulfilment?

• Jesus Christ

Christians believe that Jesus Christ provides the ultimate meaning and purpose to life.

> **S**o I say to you: Ask and it will be given to you; seek and you will find; knock and the door will be opened to you. *Luke 11:9*
>
> I have come that they may have life, and have it to the full. *John 10:10*

Christian belief
the bottom line

- God is interested in our lives and he has a purpose for our existence
- We will all face God's judgment after this life
- Jesus Christ provides the ultimate meaning and fulfilment in life

Jesus of Nazareth

• What do you know and believe about Jesus of Nazareth?

Do you believe that Jesus:

- ☐ Was born to a virgin
- ☐ Taught using parables
- ☐ Performed miracles
- ☐ Died on a cross
- ☐ Rose from the dead

How much have you read about Jesus in the Bible?

- ☐ Nothing
- ☐ Some
- ☐ A lot

Nazareth
Sea of Galilee
Caesarea
River Jordan
ISRAEL
Joppa
Jerusalem
Jericho
Bethlehem
Dead Sea

In those days Caesar Augustus issued a decree that a census should be taken of the entire Roman world. (This was the first census that took place while Quirinius was governor of Syria.) And everyone went to his own town to register.

So Joseph also went up from the town of Nazareth in Galilee to Judea, to Bethlehem the town of David, because he belonged to the house and line of David. He went there to register with Mary, who was pledged to be married to him and was expecting a child. While they were there, the time came for the baby to be born, and she gave birth to her firstborn, a son. She wrapped him in cloths and placed him in a manger, because there was no room for them in the inn.

Luke 2:1-7

What historical evidence is there for Jesus?

- **The New Testament** — the New Testament gives us most information about Jesus. There are far more early documents relating to the New Testament than to any other well-known ancient writing of the same period (eg Caesar, Homer, Plato etc). There are also many quotations and some early translations of the New Testament.
- **Other Christian writings** — we have copies of many letters and essays written by early Christians.
- **Other writings** — Jesus and Christians are mentioned by Jewish and Roman historians near the time.
- **Archaeology** — archaeological discoveries have shown that the New Testament is accurate in its geographical, historical and cultural information. There are also remains of early church buildings.
- **The existence of Christians** — the existence of Christians from the first century to the present day is itself impressive evidence.

(See chart on page 32 for more details)

Jesus of Nazareth

• Setting the scene

Jesus was born in Bethlehem to a virgin called Mary who was engaged to be married to Joseph. He was brought up in Nazareth in the north of Israel near the Sea of Galilee. Apart from a brief incident at twelve years of age, we know little about the early years of his life but as the eldest son he would have helped Joseph who was a carpenter.

When he was thirty, he was baptised by John the Baptist, a close relative. This began about three years of teaching and healing before he was eventually arrested, tried and executed at the instigation of the religious leaders.

H e went to Nazareth, where he had been brought up, and on the Sabbath day he went into the synagogue, as was his custom. And he stood up to read. The scroll of the prophet Isaiah was handed to him. Unrolling it, he found the place where is written:

"The Spirit of the Lord is on me, because he has anointed me to preach good news to the poor. He has sent me to proclaim freedom for the prisoners and recovery of sight for the blind, to release the oppressed, to proclaim the year of the Lord's favour."

Then he rolled up the scroll, gave it back to the attendant and sat down. The eyes of everyone in the synagogue were fastened on him, and he began by saying to them, "Today this scripture is fulfilled in your hearing." *Luke 4:16-21*

I n the fifteenth year of the reign of Tiberius Caesar — when Pontius Pilate was governor of Judea, Herod tetrarch of Galilee, his brother Philip tetrarch of Iturea and Traconitis, and Lysanias tetrarch of Abilene — during the high priesthood of Annas and Caiaphas, the word of God came to John son of Zechariah in the desert. He went into all the country around the Jordan, preaching a baptism of repentance for the forgiveness of sins. *Luke 3:1-3*

When all the people were being baptised, Jesus was baptised too. And as he was praying, heaven was opened and the Holy Spirit descended on him in bodily form like a dove. And a voice came from heaven: "You are my Son, whom I love; with you I am well pleased."

Now Jesus himself was about thirty years old when he began his ministry. He was the son, so it was thought, of Joseph... *Luke 3:21-23*

• What do you think of Jesus's "manifesto"?

Christian belief
the bottom line

- Jesus of Nazareth was a real man who lived in the early first century
- He was born to a virgin and conceived by the Holy Spirit

Jesus of Nazareth

• What was Jesus like?

We don't know what he looked like, how tall he was or the colour of his eyes or hair but we know a lot about the sort of man he was.

He was a man with feelings who cared for everybody he met and he was particularly concerned about the disadvantaged, the poor, the sick and the outcasts of society.

He clearly knew who he was, why he was here and what he should do.

He valued sincerity, humility, justice and honesty and bravely spoke out against the hypocrisy of the religious leaders of his time — particularly the Pharisees and the Sadducees. It was this confrontation which eventually cost him his life.

> When he saw the crowds, he had compassion on them, because they were harassed and helpless, like sheep without a shepherd. *Matt 9:36*
>
> As he approached Jerusalem and saw the city, he wept over it... *Luke 19:41*

• If you could meet Jesus, what would you ask him?

> He looked around at them in anger and, deeply distressed at their stubborn hearts, said to the man, "Stretch out your hand." He stretched it out, and his hand was completely restored. *Mark 3:5*

> When the Sabbath came, he began to teach in the synagogue, and many who heard him were amazed. "Where did this man get these things?" they asked. "What's this wisdom that has been given him, that he even does miracles! Isn't this the carpenter? Isn't this Mary's son and the brother of James, Joseph, Judas and Simon? Aren't his sisters here with us?" *Mark 6:2-3*
>
> Jesus went into Galilee, proclaiming the good news of God. "The time has come," he said. "The kingdom of God is near. Repent and believe the good news!" *Mark 1:14-15*

His style

Jesus travelled around the land of Israel teaching and healing. He taught by the Sea of Galilee, on mountains, in towns and villages, in homes, in synagogues and in the temple at Jerusalem.

He spoke about the Kingdom of God which is present wherever God is loved, served and obeyed and finally will be evident to all. He used parables from everyday life to illustrate his teachings and amazed people by his wisdom.

> When the teachers of the law who were Pharisees saw him eating with the "sinners" and tax collectors, they asked his disciples: "Why does he eat with tax collectors and 'sinners'?" On hearing this, Jesus said to them, "It is not the healthy who need a doctor, but the sick. I have not come to call the righteous, but sinners." *Mark 2:16-17*

Jesus of Nazareth

• What Jesus taught — some of his themes

• Love

Jesus taught about God's love for us and portrayed God as seeking lost mankind. He commanded us to love God and everybody in the world – including our enemies! There is no place for hate or revenge in the Kingdom of God and he laid down clear guidelines for peace and reconciliation through love, apology and forgiveness. We are to forgive as God forgives us. He made a special point of extending the forgiveness of God to those whom society considered particularly wicked. He also condemned social injustice and discrimination.

• Humility

Jesus was a humble man and encouraged humility in his disciples. He condemned pride, arrogance, self-righteousness and judgment of others. Humility before God should lead to repentance.

• Wealth

Jesus himself did not have a home or any wealth. He promoted a simple, generous way of life and warned of the dangers of greed, materialism, and accumulating wealth in this life — it is far better to store treasure in heaven!

• Sex

Jesus upheld marriage as God's institution and the appropriate setting for sexual relationships. He denounced divorce and strongly condemned adultery and immoral acts and thoughts.

• Challenge

Jesus's demands of discipleship were very challenging — everything must be subordinate to obediently serving God. His disciples should not be ashamed of him and could expect the same treatment from the rest of the world as he received — "deny yourself, take up your cross and follow me".

• Prayer

For Jesus, prayer was a living, two-way, intimate and personal relationship with his father and he inspired his disciples to develop a similar relationship. He encouraged them to worship God, to pray for God's will to be done and to ask for forgiveness. He urged them to ask God persistently for things.

• Faith

Jesus encouraged his disciples to have absolute trust in God and not to be afraid or anxious — he offered refreshment and rest for those weary of life. With faith the impossible can be achieved and faith in Jesus is the way to eternal life.

• Politics

Jesus concentrated on changing mankind from inside the individual and did not express any strong political views. He taught that we should pay our taxes and comply with the law. He was more interested in the Kingdom of God.

• The Future

He prepared his disciples for difficult times of persecution ahead. He spoke about the signs of the end of the age, his second coming, the resurrection of the dead, the final judgment of all mankind, rewards for the righteous, punishment for the wicked and final destinations in heaven or hell.

Christian belief
the bottom line

- Jesus travelled around Israel teaching and healing
- He taught about the Kingdom of God, how we should live and about himself

Jesus of Nazareth

• The cross

• Jesus's last week

- **Sunday** — He entered Jerusalem riding on a donkey.
- **Monday, Tuesday and Wednesday** — He was in Jerusalem, healing and teaching. His radical teaching antagonised the religious leaders.
- **Thursday** — Jesus had a final meal with his disciples and taught them many things. In the evening he went into a garden where he was betrayed with a kiss by Judas, one of his disciples. He was arrested and tried, first by the religious leaders.
- **Friday** — His enemies were determined to get rid of him and they presented him early in the morning to the Roman Governor, Pontius Pilate, who did not accept the charges and could find no reason to execute him. The religious leaders stirred up the people so much that Pilate agreed unwillingly to his crucifixion.

After various tortures, Jesus was nailed to a cross and he died after about six hours. Later that day he was taken down from the cross by friends and wrapped in strips of linen. His body was placed in a cave-like tomb and a stone rolled over the entrance.

• What do you think of the crucifixion — did Jesus deserve this?

The chief priests and the whole Sanhedrin were looking for evidence against Jesus so that they could put him to death, but they did not find any. *Mark 14:55*

Then Pilate took Jesus and had him flogged. The soldiers twisted together a crown of thorns and put it on his head. They clothed him in a purple robe and went up to him again and again, saying, "Hail, king of the Jews!" And they struck him in the face. *John 19:1-3*

They crucified two robbers with him, one on his right and one on his left. Those who passed by hurled insults at him...

At the sixth hour darkness came over the whole land until the ninth hour. And at the ninth hour Jesus cried out in a loud voice, "Eloi, Eloi, lama sabachthani?" — which means, "My God, my God, why have you forsaken me?"... With a loud cry, Jesus breathed his last. The curtain of the temple was torn in two from top to bottom. And when the centurion, who stood there in front of Jesus, heard his cry and saw how he died, he said, "Surely this man was the Son of God!" *Mark 15:27-39*

Jesus of Nazareth

• The empty tomb

Did Jesus really rise from the dead?

Many have tried in vain to disprove the resurrection — here are some theories:

- **Jesus did not really die** — but he was certified dead by a Roman soldier, wrapped in graveclothes and placed in a tomb — and anyway how could a man with such appalling injuries and blood loss give a convincing show of being raised?
- **The body was stolen by his disciples** — but they were so afraid and did not expect him to rise. They were basically honest people and were later persecuted for their faith; would they do this for a lie?
- **The authorities stole the body** — but why didn't they produce it again when the disciples started preaching about the resurrection?

When the disciples were together, with the doors locked for fear of the Jews, Jesus came and stood among them and said, "Peace be with you!" After he said this, he showed them his hands and side. The disciples were overjoyed when they saw the Lord.

John 20:19-20

• What is your verdict?

On the first day of the week, very early in the morning, the women took the spices they had prepared and went to the tomb. They found the stone rolled away from the tomb, but when they entered, they did not find the body of the Lord Jesus. While they were wondering about this, suddenly two men in clothes that gleamed like lightning stood beside them. In their fright the women bowed down with their faces to the ground, but the men said to them, "Why do you look for the living among the dead? He is not here; he has risen! Remember how he told you, while he was still with you in Galilee: 'The Son of Man must be delivered into the hands of sinful men, be crucified and on the third day be raised again.'"

Luke 24:1-7

After his suffering, he showed himself to these men and gave many convincing proofs that he was alive. He appeared to them over a period of forty days and spoke about the kingdom of God.

Acts 1:3

After he said this, he was taken up before their very eyes, and a cloud hid him from their sight.

Acts 1:9

Christian belief
the bottom line

- **Jesus died on a cross**
- **Jesus rose bodily from the dead on the third day**
- **He ascended into heaven**

Jesus the Christ

• Messiah?

At the time of Jesus, the Jews were expecting a political Messiah who would re-establish the Kingdom of Israel.

Jesus claimed to be the Messiah but his intentions were quite different — he came with a message of an invisible kingdom in the hearts of men, a kingdom of righteousness which is advancing and which will eventually triumph over evil.

"Messiah" is a Hebrew word
"Christ" is a Greek word
both mean **"anointed one"**

Jesus and healing

Jesus healed people of a wide variety of complaints including blindness, deafness, paralysis, leprosy, fever, internal bleeding, withered limbs and bent backs — and he raised some people from the dead! He also cast demons out of those who were oppressed.

He healed by his word of command and sometimes he laid his hands upon the sick or touched them. Healing was complete and immediate.

• What do you think about Jesus's healings?

The woman said, "I know that Messiah" (called Christ) "is coming. When he comes, he will explain everything to us." Then Jesus declared, "I who speak to you am he." *John 4:25-26*

"But what about you?" he asked. "Who do you say I am?" Simon Peter answered, "You are the Christ, the Son of the living God." Jesus replied, "Blessed are you, Simon son of Jonah, for this was not revealed to you by man, but by my Father in heaven." *Matt 16:15-17*

The high priest said to him, "I charge you under oath by the living God: Tell us if you are the Christ, the Son of God." "Yes, it is as you say," Jesus replied. "But I say to all of you: In the future you will see the Son of Man sitting at the right hand of the Mighty One and coming on the clouds of heaven." *Matt 26:63-64*

A man with leprosy came to him and begged him on his knees, "If you are willing, you can make me clean." Filled with compassion, Jesus reached out his hand and touched the man. "I am willing," he said. "Be clean!" Immediately the leprosy left him and he was cured. *Mark 1:40-42*

"But so that you may know that the Son of Man has authority on earth to forgive sins. . . ." Then he said to the paralytic, "Get up, take your mat and go home." And the man got up and went home. *Matt 9:6-7*

"I ams" of Jesus

Iam the bread of life. He who comes to me will never go hungry, and he who believes in me will never be thirsty.

John 6:35

Iam the light of the world. Whoever follows me will never walk in darkness, but will have the light of life. *John 8:12*

Iam the gate; whoever enters through me will be saved. He will come in and go out, and find pasture. *John 10:9*

Iam the good shepherd. The good shepherd lays down his life for the sheep.

John 10:11

Iam the resurrection and the life. He who believes in me will live, even though he dies; and whoever lives and believes in me will never die. Do you believe this?

John 11:25-26

Iam the way and the truth and the life. No one comes to the Father except through me. *John 14:6*

Iam the vine; you are the branches. If a man remains in me and I in him, he will bear much fruit; apart from me you can do nothing. *John 15:5*

Itell you the truth, before Abraham was born, *I am!* *John 8:58*

• *Do any of these "I ams" surprise or interest you?*

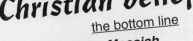

• Son of God — Son of Man

Jesus also knew that he was the Son of God with a special mission to save mankind. He had a close relationship with his father and was the perfect unspoilt image of God here on earth. On two occasions (at his baptism and the transfiguration) God himself declared in an audible voice that this was his Son!

He often referred to himself as the "Son of Man" which would be understood by his audience as the Messiah and the Son of God.

As the Son of Man, he had authority to forgive sins and work miracles and he would return in the future in a glorious manner to execute final judgment on mankind.

Christian belief
the bottom line

• **Jesus was the Messiah expected by the Jews**

• **Jesus was the Son of God**

Jesus the Christ

• Bad, mad or the Son of God?

How do we explain Jesus's astonishing claims about himself?

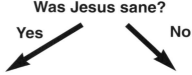

Was Jesus sane?

Yes **No**

If he was sane, was he honest?

Yes **No**

Jesus was insane, mad and deluded?

> **M**any of them said, "He is demon-possessed and raving mad. Why listen to him?" But others said, "These are not the sayings of a man possessed by a demon. Can a demon open the eyes of the blind?"
> *John 10:20-21*

Jesus was the Son of God?

Jesus was bad, a liar, a fraud, a deceiver?

> **T**hen those who were in the boat worshipped him, saying, "Truly you are the Son of God." *Matt 14:33*
> Then Nathanael declared, "Rabbi, you are the Son of God; you are the King of Israel." *John 1:49*
> "Yes, Lord," she told him, "I believe that you are the Christ, the Son of God, who was to come into the world." *John 11:27*

> **T**he Pharisees and the teachers of the law began thinking to themselves, "Who is this fellow who speaks blasphemy? Who can forgive sins but God alone?" *Luke 5:21*
> Among the crowds there was widespread whispering about him. Some said, "He is a good man." Others replied, "No, he deceives the people." *John 7:12*

But he talked so much sense. His profound moral teaching has been appreciated throughout the world (even by non-Christians) — it is not the product of a deranged mind or the ravings of a lunatic!

His friends came to the conclusion that he was the Son of God.

Others nearer the time came to the same conclusion as have millions of sincere and intelligent Christians over the centuries since then.

It is quite out of character for a man of such humility, compassion and consistency to deceive intentionally.

Would he really go as far as to allow himself to be crucified to prove his lies?

And what about the miracles — he was able to control weather and other aspects of nature — and how did he rise from the dead?

Do you believe that Jesus was:
- [ ] A good man
- [ ] Mad
- [ ] A fraud
- [ ] The Son of God

Jesus the Christ

• Jesus is eternal and one with his Father

In the beginning was the Word, and the Word was with God, and the Word was God. He was with God in the beginning. Through him all things were made; without him nothing was made that has been made...

The Word became flesh and made his dwelling among us. We have seen his glory, the glory of the Only Begotten, who came from the Father, full of grace and truth. *John 1:1-3,14*

• What do these quotations say about Jesus Christ?

The Father judges no one, but has entrusted all judgment to the Son, that all may honour the Son just as they honour the Father. He who does not honour the Son does not honour the Father, who sent him. *John 5:22-23*

I do nothing on my own but speak just what the Father has taught me. The one who sent me is with me; he has not left me alone, for I always do what pleases him. *John 8:28-29*

I and the Father are one. *John 10:30*

When a man believes in me, he does not believe in me only, but in the one who sent me. *John 12:44*

...and whoever accepts me accepts the one who sent me. *John 13:20*

Anyone who has seen me has seen the Father. *John 14:9*

He is the image of the invisible God, the firstborn over all creation. For by him all things were created: things in heaven and on earth, visible and invisible, whether thrones or powers or rulers or authorities; all things were created by him and for him. He is before all things, and in him all things hold together. *Col 1:15-17*

For in Christ all the fulness of the Deity lives in bodily form... *Col 2:9*

And now, Father, glorify me in your presence with the glory I had with you before the world began. *John 17:5*

I am the Alpha and the Omega, the First and the Last, the Beginning and the End. *Rev 22:13*

In these last days he has spoken to us by his Son, whom he appointed heir of all things, and through whom he made the universe. The Son is the radiance of God's glory and the exact representation of his being, sustaining all things by his powerful word. After he had provided purification for sins, he sat down at the right hand of the Majesty in heaven. *Heb 1:2-3*

Christian belief
the bottom line

- Jesus Christ is the eternal Son of God who came from the Father

- He is by nature God and was involved in the creation of the universe

23

Jesus the Christ

• If Jesus was the Son of God — why the cross?

You may well ask why Jesus allowed himself to be crucified and why God permitted his Son to be treated in this way?

When we look in more detail we discover that Jesus knew that he must die in this way and he did not resist arrest. The cross was the central part of his mission — and it was in God's plan and purpose to save mankind.

> **H**e then began to teach them that the Son of Man must suffer many things and be rejected by the elders, chief priests and teachers of the law, and that he must be killed and after three days rise again. *Mark 8:31*
>
> This man was handed over to you by God's set purpose and foreknowledge; and you, with the help of wicked men, put him to death by nailing him to the cross. *Acts 2:23*

• A sacrifice

God is a just judge and wrong cannot be ignored — justice must be done. Our many failings and wrongdoings deserve punishment but God provided Jesus, a perfect man, as a substitute to carry our sins.

God's love and his justice meet at the cross.

Love ✝ Justice

> **T**his is love: not that we loved God, but that he loved us and sent his Son as an atoning sacrifice for our sins. *1 John 4:10*

Sacrifices in the Old Testament

In Old Testament days (before Jesus) animals were sacrificed when people had sinned. The idea was that a pure spotless lamb or other animal died as a substitute and carried the punishment for sin. The shedding of blood was an important part of these sacrifices.

The New Testament makes it plain that these old sacrifices were just a picture of the sacrifice of Jesus.

God	God	God
Our sin separates us from God	Jesus carried our sins	The way to God is clear

What is your reaction to this meaning of the cross?

☐ Never heard of it before

☐ Hard to believe

☐ It makes sense

☐ It shows God's love

> **A**nd having disarmed the powers and authorities, he made a public spectacle of them, triumphing over them by the cross.
>
> Col 2:15

• A triumph

The cross was the greatest triumph in history:

- **Mankind's most serious problem — sin — was dealt with**
- **Our biggest enemy — the devil — was given a mortal blow**

> **Y**our attitude should be the same as that of Christ Jesus:
>
> Who, being in very nature God, did not consider equality with God something to be grasped, but made himself nothing, taking the very nature of a servant, being made in human likeness. And being found in appearance as a man, he humbled himself and became obedient to death — even death on a cross! Therefore God exalted him to the highest place and gave him the name that is above every name, that at the name of Jesus every knee should bow, in heaven and on earth and under the earth, and every tongue confess that Jesus Christ is Lord, to the glory of God the Father.
>
> Phil 2:5-11

• Body and blood

At his last meal with his disciples before he was crucified, Jesus used bread and wine to illustrate that his body would be broken and his blood shed. Christians still remember his death with bread and wine.

> **A**nd he took bread, gave thanks and broke it, and gave it to them, saying, "This is my body given for you; do this in remembrance of me." In the same way, after the supper he took the cup, saying, "This cup is the new covenant in my blood, which is poured out for you."
>
> Luke 22:19-20

• Death defeated

The mission of Jesus was completed as he was raised from the dead and returned to his father.

- **Since Jesus was the Christ, the Son of God, it was impossible for death to hold him**
- **He has opened the way to eternal life for all who believe — we too can be raised like him**
- **He is still alive at the right hand of the Father and able to help us by the Holy Spirit whom he has sent to his followers**

Christian belief

the bottom line

- *Jesus died on the cross to take away our sins*
- *Jesus is now seated at the right hand of God*

Faith

• What is faith?

You don't have to be religious to have faith — in fact we all live by faith!

> **N**ow faith is being sure of what we hope for and certain of what we do not see.
>
> Heb 11:1

Which of these do you believe?
- ☐ The earth is round
- ☐ Americans landed on the moon
- ☐ Julius Caesar existed

Why do you believe these things — what evidence do you have?

• Faith about...

There are many things in life which we have never proved ourselves but which we assume are true. Most of the things we believe and take for granted we have received second hand from other people and take their word for it.

• Faith in...

Another level of faith is **believing in** or **trusting in** something or someone. This kind of faith is required particularly when circumstances affect us personally.

It is one thing to believe that an aeroplane will fly, it is another thing to go up in the plane! To do so you put your trust in the plane designers, the maintenance engineers, the pilot, the materials which the plane is made out of etc. In the same way you put your trust in a surgeon when he operates on you!

• Faith is important

Being a Christian is not just believing things about Jesus but it is **believing in him — putting our trust in him**. Faith is the way of salvation and eternal life, as well as the way to live our daily lives. There are many levels of faith but the most important faith is the faith which saves.

• What is the faith which saves?

> **J**esus said to the woman, "Your faith has saved you; go in peace." Luke 7:50

Christian belief
the bottom line

- Having faith in Jesus Christ means putting our trust in him
- Faith about Jesus is not enough

Faith

• *Faith about God — faith in God?*

1) Faith in the supernatural

Many people believe that there is more than just this material universe — there is a spiritual realm of some sort.

> Do you have this faith? (1)
> ☐ Yes ☐ No

2) Faith that there is a creator God

There is also more specific faith that there is a God who made the universe.

> Do you have this faith? (2)
> ☐ Yes ☐ No

> **Y**ou believe that there is one God. Good! Even the demons believe that — and shudder.
> *James 2:19*

3) Faith that God can hear

Even the most unreligious people may turn to prayer in times of need and emergency in the hope that there is someone up there who is listening and who can help.

> Do you have this faith? (3)
> ☐ Yes ☐ No

> **I**n Lystra there sat a man crippled in his feet, who was lame from birth and had never walked. He listened to Paul as he was speaking. Paul looked directly at him, saw that he had faith to be healed and called out, "Stand up on your feet!" At that, the man jumped up and began to walk.
> *Acts 14:8-10*

4) Faith that God is powerful

Some have faith that God can answer prayer, intervene in the affairs of this world, perform miracles and heal the sick.

> Do you have this faith? (4)
> ☐ Yes ☐ No

5) Faith that God is loving and just

This is the God revealed in the Bible. The God who loves all mankind and wants to have a relationship with us and yet who is a God of justice who rewards righteousness and punishes wickedness.

> Do you have this faith? (5)
> ☐ Yes ☐ No

> **A**nd without faith it is impossible to please God, because anyone who comes to him must believe that he exists and that he rewards those who earnestly seek him.
> *Heb 11:6*

Belief about the existence, nature and character of God are essential to the Christian — but it does not necessarily save!

Faith

• Faith about Jesus

You may believe the facts about Jesus:

- **Jesus lived, died on a cross and was raised from the dead**

- **Jesus is the Christ, the Son of God**

But faith **about** Jesus is not the faith which saves, we need faith **in** Jesus!

Do you have this faith?

☐ Yes ☐ No

• Faith in Jesus — the faith which saves

> **H**e then brought them out and asked, "Sirs, what must I do to be saved?" They replied, "Believe in the Lord Jesus, and you will be saved — you and your household." *Acts 16:30-31*

Faith in Jesus is much more personal. It involves putting our trust in Jesus Christ as our saviour. It is not just agreeing to a statement of belief with your mind — it is believing in your heart in such a profound way that it changes your whole life.

• Personal faith

- **I realise that I need Jesus**

- **God loved me so much that he sent Jesus**

- **Jesus died on the cross to take away my sin**

- **I believe that Jesus is alive**

- **I put my trust in Jesus as my personal saviour — I am saved and have eternal life**

- **I have decided to follow Jesus and make him Lord of my life**

> **T**hat if you confess with your mouth, "Jesus is Lord," and believe in your heart that God raised him from the dead, you will be saved.
>
> For it is with your heart that you believe and are justified, and it is with your mouth that you confess and are saved. *Rom 10:9-10*

• Do you have this personal faith in Jesus Christ?

> **F**or God so loved the world that he gave his one and only Son, that whoever believes in him shall not perish but have eternal life. *John 3:16*

Why do we need to be saved?
Because we are separated from God by our sin and this has consequences in this life and the next.

• *Jesus — the only way*

The Bible does not teach that there are many ways to God. The way of the cross is the only way of salvation.

> **F**or there is one God and one mediator between God and men, the man Christ Jesus, ...
>
> *1 Tim 2:5*

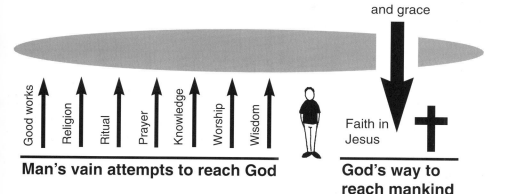

God's love and grace

Good works Religion Ritual Prayer Knowledge Worship Wisdom

Faith in Jesus

Man's vain attempts to reach God

God's way to reach mankind

• *Repentance*

Repentance is apologising to God for the things you have done wrong. It is recognising that you are a sinner and deciding to turn away from your sin. It is a place of humility where you realise that you can do nothing for your salvation and are completely dependent on the grace of God.

True repentance leads to a changed lifestyle.

> **F**or it is by grace you have been saved, through faith — and this not from yourselves, it is the gift of God...
>
> *Eph 2:8*

God's
Riches
At
Christ's
Expense

We cannot earn our salvation. We can only receive what God offers as a free gift. "Grace" is God's free gift to us.

> **E**nter through the narrow gate. For wide is the gate and broad is the road that leads to destruction, and many enter through it. But small is the gate and narrow the road that leads to life, and only a few find it.
>
> *Matt 7:13-14*

Christian belief
the bottom line

- **We are saved by faith in the Lord Jesus Christ**
- **Jesus is the only way**
- **Repentance is necessary**

Faith

• A new life

Coming to faith in Jesus is the beginning of a new life reconciled with God. It is described as being "born again", "becoming a Christian" or "receiving Jesus into our lives".

Believers are in a position to enjoy the benefits of being children of God.

> **Y**et to all who received him, to those who believed in his name, he gave the right to become children of God — children born not of natural descent, nor of human decision or a husband's will, but born of God. *John 1:12-13*
>
> Jesus declared, "I tell you the truth, no one can see the kingdom of God unless he is born again." *John 3:3*

Father

God

Son **Holy Spirit**

• The Holy Spirit

When Jesus returned to his Father, he told his disciples that he would send the Holy Spirit to be with them and other believers. The Holy Spirit can give you power to live the sort of life which Jesus taught about.

> **R**epent and be baptised, every one of you, in the name of Jesus Christ for the forgiveness of your sins. And you will receive the gift of the Holy Spirit. *Acts 2:38*

As we live by faith, obedience and the power of the Holy Spirit, we can see amazing things happen — even miracles! Also, as Christians, we belong to a huge family throughout the world — the church.

• Restored image

Jesus came to undo the results of Adam's sin. We can be gradually changed by the Holy Spirit to become more like the perfect man, Jesus. When Jesus comes again we will be transformed to be completely like him!

> **A**nd just as we have borne the likeness of the earthly man, so shall we bear the likeness of the man from heaven. *1 Cor 15:49*
>
> Listen, I tell you a mystery: We will not all sleep, but we will all be changed – in a flash, in the twinkling of an eye, at the last trumpet. For the trumpet will sound, the dead will be raised imperishable, and we will be changed. *1 Cor 15:51-52*

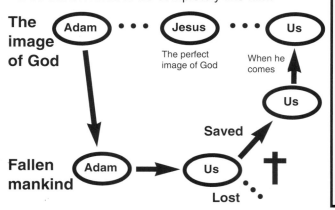

The image of God

Adam • • • Jesus • • • Us

The perfect image of God

When he comes

Us

Saved

Fallen mankind

Adam → Us

Us

Lost

30

• *Response*

Hopefully after looking through this book you have a clearer idea of what Christians believe. The Christian message, however, is not just a set of beliefs, it includes an invitation which demands a response. What is your response?

Perhaps you wish to put your faith in Jesus — in which case you could pray to God using words similar to those here. Many have come to God using such a prayer.

> **H**ere I am! I stand at the door and knock. If anyone hears my voice and opens the door, I will come in and eat with him, and he with me. *Rev 3:20*

A Prayer

- Father God, I realise that I have sinned against you.
- I apologise for my sins, I repent and turn away from them. (If there is anything obvious to you that you have done wrong — mention it to God specifically).
- I put my faith in your Son, Jesus Christ, as my Saviour. I thank you that he died on the cross for me and I receive the forgiveness available through him. I thank you that I am reconciled with you through Jesus.
- Jesus, I ask you into my life to be my Lord. Please fill me with your Holy Spirit. I want to serve you for the rest of my life.

Amen

• *Want to know more?*

There are a number of ways you can find out more:

- Read the Bible — John's gospel would be a good starting point after "Knock Knock!".
- Find a lively church with people who really believe in Jesus.
- Pray and spend time getting to know God.

Christian belief

the bottom line

- Becoming a Christian is starting a new life with God
- God sends his Holy Spirit to those who believe in Jesus
- Finally the image of God in us will be perfectly restored

Historical Evidence

BC
0
AD

Life of Jesus

Events in rest of NT

New Testament Books written

100

Existing Documents

● **P52** Earliest fragment of NT - from John

Papyrus

200

● **P66** Most of John

● **P46** Many of Paul's letters

● **P75** Parts of Luke and John

● **P45** Most of gospels and Acts

● **P47** Some of Revelation

Altogether we have about 30 separate papyri dating from before AD 300 and these contain most of the New Testament

300

● **Codex Vaticanus** Nearly whole Bible

● **Codex Sinaiticus** Whole NT, most OT

Codex

● Jerome translates Bible into Latin "The Vulgate"

400

● **Codex Alexandrinus** Whole Bible

● Syriac & Coptic translations

Other people who wrote about Jesus

Apart from the Bible, we also have writings of many other people who lived nearer the time. Some of these are Christian writers, others are non-Christian officials and historians.

Clement - Rome
Ignatius - Antioch
Polycarp - Smyrna
Justin Martyr
Irenaeus - Lyons
Clement - Alexandria
Tertullian - Carthage
Hippolytus - Rome
Origen - Alexandria
Cyprian - Carthage

● **Josephus**

A Jewish historian who mentions Jesus, his teaching, death and resurrection (about AD 90).

● **Pliny** ● **Tacitus**
● **Suetonius**

Roman officials who write about the death of Christ, the existence of Christians, their firm faith, manner of life, worship and persecution (about AD 115).

(lines indicate approx life-span)

Early writings by Christians

These early Christian leaders wrote about their faith and about their churches. There are thousands of quotations from the New Testament — in fact so many that most of the New Testament text could be reconstructed from these documents alone!

Eusebius - church historian

● **Constantine**

Constantine was converted and made Christianity a favoured religion in the Roman Empire.

● **Buildings**

Remains exist of many church buildings from this time and onwards.

Augustine

● **Canon and creeds**

The composition of the New Testament (canon) was accepted and statements of belief (creeds) were adopted around this time.